Quarter Blend Polly

Quarter Blend Polly

Poems

DANIEL FITZPATRICK
Foreword by J. C. Scharl

RESOURCE *Publications* • Eugene, Oregon

QUARTER BLEND POLLY
Poems

Copyright © 2025 Daniel Fitzpatrick. All rights reserved. Except for brief quotations in critical publications or reviews, no part of this book may be reproduced in any manner without prior written permission from the publisher. Write: Permissions, Wipf and Stock Publishers, 199 W. 8th Ave., Suite 3, Eugene, OR 97401.

Resource Publications
An Imprint of Wipf and Stock Publishers
199 W. 8th Ave., Suite 3
Eugene, OR 97401

www.wipfandstock.com

PAPERBACK ISBN: 979-8-3852-3288-8
HARDCOVER ISBN: 979-8-3852-3289-5
EBOOK ISBN: 979-8-3852-3290-1
VERSION NUMBER 01/17/25

For Grace

and for the city of New Orleans

CONTENTS

Foreword by J. C. Scharl | ix
Acknowledgments | xiii

A Birthday for Peter | 1
Oracle at Delphi | 3
Howl | 4
A Minor Directive | 5
Moriah | 6
Freedom of Expression | 7
Nguva Song | 8
This You Call Civilization | 9
Middle Passage | 10
Revery | 11
For Clementine Hunter | 12
This Is What Happens | 13
The Drunkard and the Whale | 15
Catharsis | 16
Colloquy | 17
Christchurch Meadow | 18
Sculpture Garden | 19
Landscape with Women | 21
The Magnet of Parnassus | 22
Children's Hour | 24
Memento | 25
Bernini | 27
The Death of the Student | 28
Writing | 29
Neighbors | 30

The Silk Worm | 32
The Pulpit | 33
At the Door of His Tent | 34
Flood, 2005 | 35
Jacques and Raissa | 36
Leaves | 37
Gibeah | 40
Cloak | 42
Friendship Cemetery | 43
Fox | 45
Below the Dam | 46
Once Sent to Bed | 47
Jeremiah | 48
Good News | 49
The Angel of Lligat Comes to Tampa | 51
Icarus | 52
Exile | 54
Tackle | 55
The Bridge | 57
Kandinsky at the Closing of an Eye | 59
Nostalgia | 60
The Man with the Brown Guitar | 61
Promise | 62
The Painter to His Muse | 63
St. Francis at the Turning of the Year | 64
The Altar Boys' Smoke Break in Photographs | 65
The Artists' Lament | 66
The Table | 67
Still Life With Candle | 68
What You Do Not Have | 69
Suzanne's Career | 70
Eleazar and the Elephant | 71
The Death of the Art Teacher | 72
The Kindness of Memory | 73
Conjugation | 75
Signs | 77

FOREWORD

Poetry is a topic poets love to talk about. What is it? What isn't it? Why is it important? Sometimes even, in moments of supreme self-doubt, is it important at all? These conservations are pleasant but not always productive, because the core of poetry is not a theory or an idea. It is a thing: a poem itself. Only by studying actual poems can we begin to discern what poetry is and why it matters.

That principle is also key to understanding individual poems and measuring their relative worth. A (good) poem is a window into reality, a precise linguistic account of what is. The best poems are the best accounts: the clearest, most robust, most expansive and evocative. A perfect poem is, quite simply, an account of reality so good, so true, that not a single piece of the poem (no image, no line break, no vowel sound, no comma) can be changed without alienating us from the truth.

Daniel Fitzpatrick's second volume stands as a remarkable tribute to the necessity of poetic attention to what is real. As in his first volume, Fitzpatrick is tangibly concerned with reality—not "reality" as a concept, but the reality he sees all around him, the truth of his particular time and particular place. His keen eye for particularity is a reminder of what poetry ought to be: attention to the material world, attention so rapt that it perceives the Reality *beyond* this physical reality. These are poems specific to a time and a place—21st-century southern Louisiana—composed in a specific voice—that of a devout Catholic father and husband. The tang of that curious landscape and these curious days is never absent. But the poems' very precision is what allows them to stretch across time and space. Their distinct soundwaves ping off other moments and places in human history, so that they seem to grow in the reading.

Sometimes, of course, poets strain themselves to make this move beyond, and it shows in their work. It is tempting to overleap the material real in our pursuit of the transcendent Real. Even the most mystical, the most transcendental poet must always remember that he or she is looking both *at* and *through*. A painter who is depicting a clear pane of glass cannot simply ignore it and paint only what is on the other side; instead, he must attend to the glass as well as the view beyond. Otherwise, his painting will not strike true. And, as the Dutch Masters showed, attention to something almost invisible—like glass—can unveil long-hidden beauties.

Sometimes, true attention to his subject takes Fitzpatrick to strange, almost Baudelairean scenes, where "beneath the zenith and the noon-/tide sleeps a city in malaise" and "an orchestrated horror/clasps the ringworm and the flood" ("The Drunkard and the Whale). Sometimes it leads him to comic insights, as in the poem "Children's Hour," where the children's "instinct for disaster is sublime." Sometimes the poems are incantatory, heady, surrealist visions, as in the ekphrastic "This Is What Happens," which elevates Southern slanginess to ecstatic psalmic wails ("Tell mama where it hurts now/show mama the hole/in your side. . .").

Fitzpatrick regularly invokes memorable and sensual images, but in doing so, he recognizes that he is wading into a quagmire that has trapped many a religious writer. To write with keen attention is, inevitably, to come to love *this* world, this world of dust and vanity, this world that Christians believe is passing away. Leo Tolstoy, one of the finest recorders of sense experience, came to reject his own masterpieces of *War and Peace* and *Anna Karenina* as decadent distractions from the austere truths of life. Fitzpatrick is well aware of the potential pitfalls of loving this world too much, warning in "Revery" that

> This latest blazon speaks decay, decay,
> to shake fresh garlands from the crimson dust
> and cake this vapid oracular lust
> in dewfall, moonspun, agate, anger, light,
> and make a sacred argument of night."

Fitzpatrick recognizes that religious poets are always working out the struggle between the sensual beauty of this world and the reality that all earthly things are only a few moments from decay. "Think now of what can't cross the cleansing stream," he says in "Colloquy," reminding us that even the most gorgeous images that he attends to are short-lived. But in "Christchurch Meadow," Fitzpatrick offers a defense of the sensual world; with all its insufficient beauties, it yet serves "to whet/that hunger for the hidden sun."

The poems themselves are a blend of recognizable traditional forms, including sonnets and terza rima, loosely rhymed and/or metered verses, and delicately ghost-metered free verse. Fitzpatrick's range demonstrates the very best of the contemporary American poetry world, in which skill with traditional forms can flourish alongside a mastery of the subtle art of free verse, and provides a pleasing sense of the simultaneously structured and unstructured nature of the reality to which the poems bear witness.

For example, "Flood, 2005," an homage to the survivors of Hurricane Katrina "returned to a Lazarus world," is written in subdued tetrameter. The four feet of each line slip along, sometimes stumbling, occasionally almost vanishing, then reappearing with a sense of self-discovery, even as the survivors in the poem rediscover their old world buried beneath the debris of the flood. The poem ends on a perfect iambic tetrameter line, "began to be as we had been," promising that life can go on even after disaster.

This volume of poetry is not perfect; occasionally I found the poems a little florid and overgrown, a few of the details distracting. But that is the risk we run when we attend closely, and Fitzpatrick has dared greatly. I am willing to take a few extra leaves and flowers as the price for the kind of true affection for reality that we find in these poems—affection that draws us not only to love what is, but also what is beyond.

ACKNOWLEDGMENTS

Thanks are due to the editors of the following journals, who first gave many of these poems their homes: Antiphony Journal ("The Oracle at Delphi"), Poems for Persons of Interest ("Howl"), Voegelin View ("Revery"), Shadowlands Dispatch ("Christ Church Meadow"), Ekstasis ("The Death of the Student"), New Verse Review ("Neighbors," "Tackle"), Catholic 365 ("The Bridge"), Eunoia Review ("Promise"), Surely as the Sun ("The Altar Boys' Smoke Break in Photographs"), Spirit Fire Review ("The Death of the Art Teacher"), Voice and Virtue ("The Table," "Exile," "This Is What Happens"), Loblolly ("Signs," "Conjugation," "Moriah"), Ranger ("Freedom of Expression," "Bernini," "The Painter to His Muse"), Litmora ("Middle Passage," "Kandinsky at the Closing of an Eye"), The Ekphrastic Review ("For Clementine Hunter"), Illuminations of the Fantastic ("Colloquy"), Beneath the Garden ("The Pulpit," "Suzanne's Career"), Glass: Facets of Poetry ("At the Door of His Tent"), Hooghly Review ("Leaves"), Foreshadow ("Cloak," "Jeremiah"), Forgotten Ground Regained ("Fox"), Trampoline ("Good News," "The Angel of Lligat Comes to Tampa")

A BIRTHDAY FOR PETER

There once were bells
downriver in the night.
Did the ghosts of them toll
as you swept back
our simple winter's
alabaster blue
etched on high
in swallowtails?
For you the first of days
is shorter than the rest
in the sun-dimmed world
where you kick and wriggle
like the shape we watched
in awe, the shadow
in your mother's skin.
These twenty-three hours
of the doctored clock
echo her exultant shrieks,
naked, four-legged, muting
the sin scream to Eden
felt fleetly in this flesh of
flesh of my death
in the dark of June,
twice-backed, shelled together
to the frigid moon-sweep,
to the flooded world,
to you, brave grit-gleam

in the prodigal night.
Once the bells pieced out
our primal sympathy,
the chanted waves
reticulate with grace.
We cannot see
the dark desirous water
in this silence.
We cannot see
for the city
and the levee
the low ship breasting
the splendid ooze
of our continent.
But there sail the cross trees,
one, two, three,
through the silence
of the steeples
in their sleep.

ORACLE AT DELPHI

Down the shade slope cupping waves unsunned,
no grape pulp breaking but the wineblack
plum's blood swells, dimpled copper of cloud splay.
The road shrine glares in the grove
of loose-hipped dogwood, moon-blotting.
Rose furls feather upper air.
Corinth Sea couples columns
as blood, sporting with porpoises,
breasted blind Tiresias trembling with wand-touch,
angelic verge, Jesse stump striking bloom
fruit flower in one, juice-cut licking cedar, olive, cypress.
"Have you come again among the dead?"
"Have you come?"
"Have you come again?"
Three times the sword-dimmed limbs attempt
the bull neck, mugitus, staggering the vine-row.
Then flesh, agony, froth, ferment.
Up sun-edged hill hang hecatombs, fat intact,
blood-bleating, curl-horned, with desiccated cud.
Sun's deep silvers altar veins till
sacrifice repairs to pasture, sleeps—
give sorrow up to time.

HOWL

You heard it first, that loneliness aloft
against the purblind sky, the certain, soft
advance of six coyotes through the oaks.
We shrank, admiring how the moonlight smoked
upon that song, how the scavenged reek shone
and shrouded those sleek ghosts of tongue and bone.
That night you'd taught me how to see the past
as part of what was promised us at last.
You touched my throat and whispered they were gone,
and soon we too arose and soon went on,
hunched against the cold without a word
for future griefs the hounds had overheard.

A MINOR DIRECTIVE

Drifting into its original rage,
the squalor of an unbegotten age
breeds banishment, abandon, and decay:
evolution with a view to dismay
and to persist in its impertinent
muttering. Our mild-mannered stuttering's
worn away its idiotic patience,
monstrous with a many-tongued fluttering.
The embers of an impious decree
cement the mettle of its mystery.
Deep inherits deep. Song inherits song.
We'll neither score nor orchestrate for long
until a pentecostal tenderness
returns, elides, elucidates our need
to shake three centuries of sleeplessness,
to take—a word of certain good—and read.

MORIAH

Go out and scale the rock that is
the locus of your call. The fire
and the knife, the curl-horned ram
await you. Perhaps you will not see them.
Perhaps for many years of bending
to the burnt or frozen stone
their presence will announce itself
by things as unassuming as a bruised knee,
an elbow scratched in rigid sleep,
a moan shucked over the slithering sands.
When you run a hand across your neck
and feel the growth that's bought
your brother's birthright,
when you learn how sharp a thing the body is,
how near blood rushes to the thundering sun,
it's still conceivable that nothing should arrive
to overwhelm you, that the absence
that rewards your fast will tear the veil
concealing all the demons who've assailed you
since you twisted, purple, screaming, from the dark.

FREEDOM OF EXPRESSION

Take a watchband for a thigh.
Lift your clasped acrylic fingers
to a sky sponged on to dress
your naked wounds. Lie down
where the surf beads up and let
the cowries clam you in the key
of incandescence. Queens of Egypt
clamor at your skirt. Can a timepiece
run to silence speak the sun's eclipse?
Curl up like the primrose by the beach.
Keen the unstrung song that spins linked
fingers into heart's blood, spattering
the calendar. There are wings now
erupting from the egg shell skin
along her spine, spreading on the air,
on the water, filling up with light.

NGUVA SONG

The small night saw you slip up
dripping dugong from the surf,
sand crazed, craving the salt-lipped flesh
of the sea cow whose companionship consumes you.
Caper up the tessellated steps and keen
your innocence to minarets. Their stillness
makes mockeries of water thoughts,
sparks up every ritual to infamy.
Now the tide-turn grooves your trust,
scans how many times your faith
can wind around the unstilled world
while mended nets tremble at your touch,
your sight slipping down, down, down
into the disappointing riches of the sea.

THIS YOU CALL CIVILIZATION

Beneath his weight and mine
against the motion of the ship
let slip from his unfeeling frantic love,
I learned to see the gulls
flow up the waves and down,
to cry the man-of-war slanted
on the storm winds in our wake.
They do not sing the manic sun.
They do not spot the leopard of the sails,
dragging up the hands who drag her up
to blot the wounded rainbow of the night.
Row, I hear from the drunken pillow.
Row, I hear them crying in the cold
of sickness creeping up beneath the deck,
of gold coins blinking into silence
on the sea's breast curdling to foam.

MIDDLE PASSAGE

There are stars like flowers on the flood.
Watch the jaws come glittering into view
to fish them, splay them ragged
on the blind back of our horror.
Have you packed the stars in smoldering rows
to unconceive the longing they excite?
Lock the roses in your cabin.
Feed that element where seeing founders.
Have they blinded you?
And did you dream that stars could steel your eyes?
Expect the nightmare oozing puckered
and spined from the dregs of your consignments.
Lift your head and graze that last
mosaic cloud quilted to conceal yourself
from you as the ship's wheel lashed
to your swollen wrists lurches
and creaks toward this tale
we tear aside so we can sleep.

REVERY

And when at last the least light sings its sleep
and mutes itself against the whirling deep
where stars fold up in friezes from the dark
like paper spirits brought before the spark
of God's insistent, incandescent dreams,
the upstart sand's recalcitrance still gleams.
These cavities of malice crease the cold
awaiting brazen instruments that hold
our cracked and trickling fingers to the chords
and conjure dreams of elemental hordes
we no more know by sleep than self by day.
This latest blazon speaks decay, decay,
to shake fresh garlands from the crimson dust
and cake this vapid oracular lust
in dewfall, moonspun, agate, anger, light,
and make a sacred argument of night.

FOR CLEMENTINE HUNTER

Strung gourds choke up out of earth, out
from loam the tinge of ecstasy at dusk.
Eyes filmed over prophesy in smoke
as cyclopes score a music of mule sweat,
chink the blackest eaves with cooled off
Sun's blood, blinking come, caution.

Ripple, crumble, fade, aching
over barrow handles,
bandanaed, powdered, stewing
a week's caked vestments far from shade.
The grass is green with killing,
the scalded earth watered with pig shrieks
spilled from the black, oak-shrouded cauldron
where unease curls in whispers,
smiling to vine the lustrous pickets.

Do not let the earth undo what dares,
slide splayed and craving from the furrow
that is yours. Let the little bites
chime the garden gate and teach
a song too deep for melody.
That's us in the ground, in the ground, crying.

THIS IS WHAT HAPPENS

After *Yo Mama*, Wangechi Mutu

This is what happens
when you strike at this
heel, at
his heel,
like a nail dragging back
your supple, severed nakedness
across the universe begotten,
born, and murdered since
we whispered each to each
between the palms gone blue
with burnt out suns.
This is what I wear,
what clings of skinned,
furred, half-eaten things
skittering in silence
between beats of my leaned-
back body hung with half-moons.

Tell mama where it hurts now
show mama the hole
in your side
let her kiss it
let her hold you close
lean your broken self
on her shoulder

let her
this is how the king's men
couldn't put him back to
go get her, get mama,
tell her where say this
is how it hurts
when you strike
at her heel.

THE DRUNKARD AND THE WHALE

Soon the wasting dewfall lies
to drench my slumber from the moon.
Through the corn a whisper flies.
Between the zenith and the noon-
tide sleeps the city in malaise.
Seven awful centuries
have slipped. The dream of hell decays.
The holy angels' injuries
have bred the sunken marble's blood.
An orchestrated horror
clasps the ringworm and the flood.
The weevil and the borer
steep their passion in demise
while down the shining river sweeps
the springtime hatch of flies.
I hear them singing in the deep,
the drunkard and the whale.
They revel in a swollen June
and pinch behemoth's tail.
His dreams are drowning, drowning soon
and still the silence swells,
and still the sickly witness sings
the words that stir the bells.
The prophets, priests, and folded wings
have touched the drooping sun
that skates along our crackling sky
and wakes us when we've once begun
to see, to hear, to die.

CATHARSIS

The red and yellow wrecker jerks its chrome
snout aside as we mount the final rise,
hooks a blue sedan in the reedy ditch,
pulls it from the nameless purple blossoms
as we coast into our valley, slowing
to see what sickness we've eluded now.

Ulysses' ship is beached on the mind's loom,
drawn out of the whirl of wanting to know.

E poi the corn beyond the moldered band
of blackberry, dogwood, hidden morel
rustles as ragged beards bent over oars
below stars at the bottom of the world.

The slow curve doubles, crosses saddled streams.
Cattle bow to sun shoots plump underfoot.
A red-tailed hawk processes in the curl
of turkey vultures turning in the light,
waiting to fan the faces of the dead.

COLLOQUY

Come now, clean and melancholy dove.
Quit the unsung water of their anguish.
Speak low, and let the rumored beats above
upbraid the bitter cities which languish
in an agony of awful musing.
Slip beneath my shoulder now. Slit my side.
Sip this ingemminate life to infuse
you with you as you had been till the pride
of the beautiful firedrake flecked your eyes.
Think not of what can't cross the cleansing stream,
but touch that chain that sounds the deepest skies,
knowing nothing is as nothing ever seems.
Peace—this sorrow's piercing sweetness remains,
converting ampler griefs by simpler pains.

CHRISTCHURCH MEADOW

Around the meadow where the pheasants stirred
the yellow grass of summer, where a word
or two at intervals of hours meant
fresh continents of wonder as we bowed
our heads like flowers with the wind, we went
at arm's length, dreaming monuments. Aloud
you simply spoke the willow and the swan,
the stream that coupled every image on

the black, stately mirror of its silence.
The red-ribbed cows appeared beyond the fence,
the swept grass breaking on them where they hulked
like wrecks of treasure ships in silhouette
against the gold cliffs of Christ Church, their bulk
submerged to gnaw our restlessness, to whet
that hunger for the hidden sun that gives
a mordant savor to the heart by which we live.

SCULPTURE GARDEN

Sit with me a while.
Breathe again,
when you can.
Learn to take
the adamant silence
of the earth and sky
and set them
in a golden floating
of flesh, of skin,
of rock that knows
the beat of human blood,
that took a pulse
from the hands of love.
There is nothing
you must do to win
the Sun's affection.
Feel the cool fire
of the god-cradling grass.
You yourself are jeweled
with morning dew,
dawn-bearded like the oaks
the wind and rain
have shaped in aching
arcs of triumph
and lament.
Rest easy in
this dream made flesh,

rest easy in your own
ecstatic suffering.
Rest easy in yourself
turned to stone.

LANDSCAPE WITH WOMEN

Women rise with infants, riddled from stone
by centuries of unrecorded rain.
Colossal on her crocodile comes
a matron through the mist, pregnant again.

It's her twelfth time now, and still she's smiling.
These years and years of interrupted sleep
can't keep sweet mischief's eyes from beguiling
time with timeless secrets. When the dark deep

sleeks on in swag-bellied rites and ruts, think
how tenderly the world's gorgeous burden
rests on these profoundly threatened shells, link-
ing claw to claw against the thought that stirred when

Sun first peeled the shadows from the sea floor.
We love the things we love for what they were.

THE MAGNET OF PARNASSUS

"And every poet has some Muse from whom he is suspended, and by whom he is said to be possessed..."
—PLATO, *ION*

I'd come down to leave the Sun
and sleep for once in the shade.
I crossed the meadow where the
orange-banded grasshoppers
clattered like magnolia leaves
down dry stream beds in the breeze.
Moonflowers' lemon odor
flowed over the roots and woke
me. I heard the trout sipping
mayflies, stretched, and bent above
a gravel pool. From the depth
reflected rose an oak limb,
rippling like the light I'd seen
caressing the secret green
of spiracles. Deeper still
appeared, like beads swinging strung
upon a broken chain or
acrobats magnetic with
their magical act, faces
falling toward the blue darkness.
Closest rose my grandmother,

copying a Matisse, paint
in tendrils dripping slow arcs
ascending to the Spaniard's
left palm scarred in the staring
shape of an eye. The other
etched out pigeons in the air.
They wheeled away applauding
Dickinson as Whitman held
her by the blinding ankles,
while above both in a whale
boat Artemisia spoke
with Socrates of corpses
en route to the Piraeus.
Dante heard them sailing past
and glared, ruffling his laurel
wreath and then remembering
Vergil's political gaze.
Last a naked arm gave birth
to words that rained on the rest,
set in motion by that face
eternally turned from me
to the dark beyond images.
I stood and traced a way again
among the moonflowers, my hand
twitching imitations of that
blind hand moving in the deep.

CHILDREN'S HOUR

Their instinct for disaster is sublime.
Watch them frolic barefoot in summer grass,
and see how fast they smear their soles in pass-
ing through that clover patch where, every time
you mow, you find the moldering cat turds.
Watch how every corner, each swollen root
leaps out to meet a golden head or foot.
Feel how little force remains in the words
you fling across the yard to save yourself,
for that's the truth their carelessness reveals,
the death their ecstasy bids us accept:
ours, there, beyond the continental shelf
of desire, summoning blood to heal
that rift in love the living never left.

MEMENTO

You said that
this was where
you came
to remember
what it's like,
to show yourself again
how good it feels to
hang the bright mechanics
of your life—
the way a shrike
impales a horny toad,
you said—
and skip along
the burning sands
and drift beyond
your way of being
in the world, away
from days and nights
and Sun's dust,
away from above
and away from below,
away from yet to be
and having been.

You did not say
away from me.

You said the high tide
tempted you to see
the soul existed
not inside you
like a phantom
at the bellows
of your glands
but as the music
of your organism
drawn along
the cosmic dark
in the carnival
of the turning world.

You said you never saw
your mother step
into the water
and that you woke
to her shrieks from the shore
and swam for land,
certain you were drowning.

You said you wouldn't mind
that tide like a deep breath
sipped across a cold blue beard
and that when all the rest was lost,
it, at least, would be there,
implacable and sunless and smiling.

I tried to say
that you were right
but
       the seawater
silvering your skin
said the time
had not yet come.

BERNINI

The dimples up her thigh are like
the ghosts of Pluto's fingers
in the screaming, clawing marble
in the room across the ocean.
In the grove of pines
where afternoon is fading
the dark god sinks his hands
and feels his eye drawn out
like a drop about to fall
from the faucet, gathering itself
and stretching toward
the wet shining tiles,
feels his face stretched like
a balloon a child hugs
to her naked chest,
squeezing the color from it
as her skin shows clearer, clearer,
less and less red until
she stands clutching the dark shreds
and spreads her hands
and then her arms
and stares in silence at the floor until
she laughs
as she looks up at you.

THE DEATH OF THE STUDENT

When purple clusters pale and strew my mind
in memories of vineyard, well, and grove,
there follows ineluctably behind
the thought of him whose heart, too merry, dove
from off the pink brick Belvedere's sill
and drew a lovely body to its end.
A friendly horror rises like the shrill
of god wings folded, furious, descend-

ing to snatch back one who should have borne
the cup of sacred nectar to his lips.
The veil dividing time from time is torn.
A blessing brims the pool of curses, trips
down shell on shell of Latium's light and braids
a tender grace of death and distant seas,
of wine and one who once in purple laid
his sceptered stench against the rustling breeze.

WRITING

You pretend what you could do without it,
how every page of Plato would commend
its genius to your own, how time would send
you to eternity having doubted,
with St. Thomas, all the words that flouted
your best hopes, having followed to the end
the arguments that vanish at the bend
of reason's stream. You'd know all about it,
having no more felt the need to set words
to aching thoughts, to put the sentence down
unread and rush off after remnant song.
If only we were molded like the birds
whose beauty breaks unscripted from the ground
to swell a stranger's gaze and glide along.

NEIGHBORS

A night heron, juvenile,
lights out from its power line,
starts the crow from the roof peak.
A plastic owl overpeers tomato plants,
browning with this miserable June.

Now the heron's landed on a phone line
with a background cloud Dalí let slide
from one of his gigantic canvases
in the course of an afternoon like this,
when the heron on the string swings
back and forth at the hips like a toy,
like a man who's fallen out of a dream
onto a tightrope, unable to wake up.

He's in his eighty-second year,
the neighbor with tomatoes and a plastic owl
and the cucumber blooms I forgot to mention,
still strong, with muscles slung
from his arms in cords that come taut
when he hangs a potted snake plant from his carport
or grips and shakes his compost barrel
by the handles.

                He's had to order red worms
from a Pennsylvania farmer these three summers.
Before that he'd go home one weekend

West of Lafayette and thrum
two sticks in the syrup earth
and watch half in horror as they squelched
into the dark above the dark.
Like Isaiah's bones, he said,
knowing I knew what he meant.
Now he cannot see, and hates to hear
his grandson shriek and watch him stoop
to pluck up nothing after nothing
from the dead level ground.

He told me this and tipped the barrel toward me.
Down among the coffee grounds, the wilted
leaves of grass, the curls of apple peel
I watched them worry into view and out—
hundreds of them, thousands, quivering as one,
like the background music of the universe.

See, he said, nothing, and shut it.
Then he left us, and the painted pelican of cedar
slapped between the storm door and the dark.

THE SILK WORM

Through September's goldening green
        stretched between
the white ash and the water oak,
a silk worm humped his scrunched-up inch
        pinch by pinch
along a line my eyes' touch broke

or should, so light it looked, have broken.

        I took as token
of nature's sort of self-consumptive yearning
that it labored lash by lash
        toward the ash

cut out for this year's burning.

THE PULPIT

Below me hang the waves in their array,
stilled in ceaseless cresting, cupping
to my desperate breath those souls
who trust themselves to the curling wood.
I feel the breaking in my boots,
hear the gull calls crazing the Sun's face.
On every hand the eyeless dead
thrust up the green brine of their grave.
I see them streaming into deeper darks,
oozing down the crush of mountain slopes
to let the angel kraken cut
dead letters from their brows
as the shadows of the restless ships
oared on to newborn stars by withered men
flicker out against our world's undying night.
Their patience breaks against me,
braids our fearing and our madcap courage
as the palm whispers and the coral spreads
and time steams into our fleet
assuring us a world without us comes.

AT THE DOOR OF HIS TENT

And how not to abstract myself from me?
I find my mind exists from word to word.
I look around and I am what I see.

I shadow silver tails up ancient trees
to chatter songs the symbols have obscured.
It's easy to abstract myself from me.

I drone the bee's blue honeyed symphony
and marvel down the marbled ways of worms.
I look around and I am what I see.

I stare to hear the studied homily
but lose myself in worlds I hadn't heard.
It's easy. To abstract myself from me

Is but to be by this mortality.
The senses' science was the first to stir.
I look around and I am what I see.

This vision seals my sight's ascendancy.
Now go, bring back a steer and rolls and curds.
It's easy to abstract myself from me.
I look around, and I am as I see.

FLOOD, 2005

And some returned to a Lazarus world,
to the streets their steps had memorized,
to the ceilings aloft in the fingering mold
and the deck chairs knuckled under ivy.
The key's teeth, they were amazed to find,
still turned the warm, west-facing locks,
and a stench swelled in the kitchen and spread
into the yard and the street and the mountains
of couches and decanters, the china and the novels
and the cabinets and the tea sets stacked
to an implacable sky to say that this
was all they could remember having been.
And the cleared trees ceded the sun
their teeming heavens, and the hammers bit,
and the bones of fish brushed blossoms
from the myrtles' bones where the ants
burned in their building and we
began to be as we had been.

JACQUES AND RAISSA

Who could begin but by mentioning the chestnuts
fluttering on the margin of the leaden sketch
of the Belle Époque beyond the awning?

There they vowed their suicide—
there where swung the confident rods
questioning the Seine—should reason not appear.

Behind her in the arid gloom
sprawled Russia on diaspora's edge.
Light drank the liquid chill.

Spinoza whispered. The ox saw all straw.
Death descended quickly as the idols
flailed Verlaine, Saint-Saens, Lautrec.

Seeming rushed upon them in space
above the brazen gypsum of Montmartre
where gods awaited their salvation,

blind to the rut beneath their flicking tails,
gleefully gazing on the prospect of Verdun
and the miles of signs to Disneyland.

LEAVES

It is tempting, when an oak leaf
falls into your empty cup
as you walk to your minivan
at the end of another day's teaching,
to consider everything that had to happen
for that to happen. I do not advise it.
You will have to begin with finishing
the bottle of whisky last night
and having to park in the far lot this morning.
Even before that, though, there's the fact that
you left the other cup, the one you usually use,
in the van the day before yesterday. Of course,
you only started bringing that one because
the one in your hand today, the one with the leaf,
fell six weeks ago in the parking lot and cracked.
At any rate, you had the right cup and parked
in the right place and now at the end of the day you
decided to leave ten minutes early
because you were sitting in the dark in your classroom
trying to read a papal encyclical waiting for a call
from a mortgage company and you just couldn't take
it anymore. You slowed down to tell two students
hello. Let that suffice, (it doesn't, though, does it?)
for you, but what about this leaf, which fell
as your front foot hit the bridge over the little creek
that got just enough rain last week
to keep alive the ant that took a bite

from the leaf's left side so that
it would spin neatly into your cup? What about that ant
and the other ant that chewed the stem a second
and the squirrel that slipped and kicked the stem
and the gust of wind that did not
(now we're into the nots) blow because
an autocrat scratched his balls
and thought better of leveling Chicago?
You can go back to the night
your grandmother and grandfather went dancing
and came home and kept dancing
and couldn't believe the sun was there
to wave their friends goodbye.
You can go back to the old fear you have of cats
which started when a strand of DNA
that would become you
in 25000 years was startled
by a saber tooth tiger.
You can, when you meet this leaf, try at last
to see whether you are the sort of person
who can buy a house in this economy
or whether you are, as you have always
known yourself to be, a failure,
laughing off a lifetime's bad decisions
in verses dragged as badly to death
as that horse-haired fool below
the orphaned walls, in—it's a boy,
for the 3479th time—
not counting the twenty years of words
and the six or seven thoughts
which could have been something
if for once you'd gotten off your ass.
You can do all that, certainly,
or you can go home in the sunshine
and walk below the palms
quivering with sunshine

and kiss your wife and kiss
your children and pour some whisky
into your cup, watching the oak leaf
swirl in the sweet amber like sunshine, and sip
and watch the sunshine shake on the palms
and on the lake where the ducks have come to sleep
and think damn if this isn't delicious.

GIBEAH

A cold coming then again,
borne back from Bethlehem a second time.

Her lips dried in the journey out
after feasts and the many days' dance
of bulls slipping in their siblings' blood,

and now came cold on her father's hailing him
again, bearing wineskins toward the horizon,
rejoicing in her concubinage.

Chill settled with his eyes' reptilian urgings
morning on morning to stay, feast, sleep,
as though assembling some revenge.

Late despite those same devices,
too late they left for the depth of Ephraim.

Jerusalem arose at dusk. The mules
against the servant's word and the cold
eyes recessed pressed for Benjamin.

In Gibeah's lights the Levite
waited in the square as its eyes amassed
muttering, running wrists along their robes.

They caught her up cold still in their euphoria
before the door, dismissing the virgin mistress.

The night outraged her
and cast her on the dawn
grasping at the threshold.

Full morning found her, eyes spread
like a sturgeon's he'd slaughtered once
and tossed into the rushes.

Cold out of Judah into Ephraim's depth again.
The same blade as set the bulls staggering
carved as it could a bloodless lip,

a belly, a calf, till each tribe held her,
aghast at all since Egypt's excellence,
assembling against the one once known
as Ben Oni and beloved.

CLOAK

"When he heard this, Elijah hid his face in his cloak and went out and stood at the entrance of the cave."

—1 KINGS 19:13

The silence slithered in,
trailing its raspberry flood,
and he wrapped the spattered cloak
about his head and trembled into the air
to be dismissed by fire.

It is column of cloud and pillar
and falling flame consuming
soaked slices of bull. It is
no fingered hand plucking Pharaoh's bloom.

It is that descending on the frenzied
priests clenching the blood beat between teeth,
that look the last one turns
when the four hundred forty-ninth has fallen
and the prophet and the wadi are one.

It is the heavy rain anxious
to erase its own vermillion spoils
and the terror bowed upon Tabor and it
is that echo at last: "Eli . . ."

FRIENDSHIP CEMETERY

Not neat, in rows, winking up and down
a paved neighborhood of marble, slate.
A scattering of hillside stones like soldiers
struck attempting a ridge, stones smoothed
level with their chiseled names.
A rutted track of gravel rises, vanishes
in trees. Three picket crosses, whitewashed,
loom like totems to ward away the road,
which curves in time with the creek
and its trail of joggers, leashed dogs,
and children waving fishing rods
despite what they can see, namely,
limpid, skinny water, shimmering with shiners,
a moderately busy byway, and the worn
teeth of grey gravestones gathered
in crops of grass haphazardly shorn.
They see the sign at the intersection,
its end angling toward them: April 3, 1924.
They see daily the ivy's red deepen
up the trunk of the pine, as if bearing
a blood offering to the sun. They see earth eaten
away by rain at the slab heads jutting
above roots where chipmunks rustle.
Cypresses rise above the segregated dead,
and around one pitiless, illegible rock
stand planters draped with withered stems.
A shock of orange mums trembles

when the dump trucks strike the pothole below.
Next month, poinsettias, red wrapping
flickering into spring like temple flame, eternal.

FOX

Down the draw toward the water
where the duck have flocked,
the stones stink with riots
of fox sign. The tortured mesquite
urge us to the wigeon, pintail,
blue-winged teal tuning their whistles.
At our rising from the last rock
they leap like rain returning. We shoulder
guns, begin to brush them from
the egg shell dusk: cave dwellers
whitewashing the walls of our hides.
A teal's crescent cheek shines
in the game bag's shadow. Back up
the brittle course four lengths of shot,
we settle at the scrub oak's feet.
Dimpled walnut strokes the cracked
tip of my thumb. The dead rabbit's record
screams into a cedar copse
beyond stones like steps into the night,
and that hideous, carnal bark comes
to say how far from home we are.

BELOW THE DAM

She is in to her knees and bends and brushes
out reflected trees with both hands, then turns
to squint up at me through drops she's slapped
into her eyes. The dam drizzles on our right,
and the clear, devious flow bottoms in stocked
rainbow trout. Never turning from the current,
they weave in line where the tumble
of golden stones levels. She reaches through
herself, selects a rock, and flings it, feet
fixed. The ripples drift past, broadening
to touch a butterfly straining the surface.
Wet wings flex, lever thorax, spread again,
struggling down into the deathbed, staining
the bottom with blue shadows. She points,
and the fish flare, angling for mid river.

ONCE SENT TO BED

The light below my bedroom door
fills with voices rising as chairs rasp
their cello notes and my mother
laughs and says she's sorry again,
wineglass stems slotting the wide
webbing of her fingers, which whiten
and mute the chiming bowls nested
immovably in her palm. Her own
rings deepest, absent the egg white
residue. Brazen, the priest
blares thanks. Then the door,
and my father chuffs down steps
of brick. The picket gate scrapes
the slope of the walk (I imagine
as they slip beyond hearing),
and he waits in the dark of the Indian
Bottlebrush. His knuckles arch
the pockets of his jeans, and his
thumbs caress the loops of his belt.

JEREMIAH

Down again to bleed the Nile.
No city, no city now
for me, no city almost since
they slung me in the mire
and the Ethiopian's ropes
burned me from the cistern.
Out again to tell the king
what no one will believe.
No one will believe,
no one will,
that he will die.
No one will
believe. Did they eat, did
they drink, were they
merry. Their guts were iron.
I put a tattered cloth
to tattered loins and heave
through the beloved city, vomiting.
These words are death to me,
the death my stillborn blood
cannot abide. Too alive. Too
long living now no city
but this murmur from the river
bleeding evening, morning,
the sixth day. My belly
is content. I will lie down and
sleep, yes, yes, sleep,
yes.

GOOD NEWS

There, that twinge, that's Barnard's star
stitching up my side. Last week
it was the Crab Nebula in my ears.
Can solar wind shake the hidden garden,
let fall with all the cosmic flood
beating upon our heads the seeds to ask again
who are we to ask again who
put the word in whose mouth?
Show me the reindeer's words.
Let me see seeing.
Stand outside the theory, then the theorizer,
then see who's laughing.
Help me, Carl Sagan.
You're our only hope. As if
the cosmic heart skipped every beat
between the fire at Alexandria
and the finger of Galileo.
Thing: a walrus ivory carving of a man
and bear wheeling arm in arm
for death. Fact: this is a lie.
Bear has always already won. Fact: bear
leaves no monument to his defeat,
no thing to ponder as salmon strips
cure in the sun at the door of the cave.
Chatter on in orbit.
Admire these dyadic energies.
And all the while who is that

looking back from the window
of that craft bound for Pluto?

THE ANGEL OF LLIGAT COMES TO TAMPA

There is bread in a basket
and then a bear and a gazelle.
I am angelic, inclined to help in quiet
just to make the world a better place,
you know, for my children's children.
I am awaiting a glimpse. Wait
till she turns a little, just a little
more to the right and
I am a cormorant hulking at the peak
of a gazebo. I swim with gators
like a nightmare
and the sun dries my wings. I turn
my back on it, and my yellow charnel mouth
is cracked, pointing to the jacarandas.
I am of all most pitiable, of all
most gosh darn magnificent. Yes, that's true.
Often I pretend to be a farmer but today
I've mounted an especially violent assault
on my frontal cortex, having just sent Benjy
back the way he wants to go around the square.
America is drooling happiness.
America is up against it.
America does not know what to say
but that, of course, has never been
the problem.

ICARUS

I

And the stink of pigeons
melted into onion into oil
shearing from the Cretan kitchens
and the slow beat of Cretan sun
threshing up the crocus and anemone,
peony and orchid and the musing breath
of noon in cypress, plane, and eucalyptus
and the Cretan palm flickering
beside the sea of all longing
and then the sea itself
heaving unhurriedly its treasured dead
upon the unintending shore.

His own quick odor clung an hour
to his corner of the cell
and died untasted on the shaken sea
as his father sailed on toward
the faltering sun, collapsing
on an unknown shore,
too worn to lift his head
to the menace of this
at last this freedom,
burying his face
in the pigeon feathers
curdling in the surf.

II

And the waves slipped by below
and the being above below the air
was as the being above below the sea
that was wherever he was the being that was his
when the wings rode gravity's back
and the air streamed out in bubbles
rushing up to die upon the waves
that were themselves when the air
that was the silver office of life
undid itself becoming what it was
as sea upheld him artlessly
between the waves and the shadows of the waves
between the sun on the waves and the
not sun slithering the sea floor
and he closed his eyes and opened them
and watched the silver worlds his fingers
set sailing from his hair
spin to their unsilvering in themselves
against the sun like a lover on the waves
that spread themselves to catch what had been him
now not him bubbling up against the sun
to sink into the grief that was his beginning
soaring on toward an unknown shore.

EXILE

My morning way lay moist in hyacinth.
Day intruded on my body like a beacon
to the nodding watch upon the ramparts.
This is what we live for, yet we pray,
deep in love with Lot's life, Lord,
let it not, O, let it not, Lord, happen
in our day.
                    When we lay beneath the cedar
on the hilltops, dizzy with the hawks
against the unembarrassed noon, did you
as I did dream again the words we once let
trickle stillborn from our tongues?
The lemon seed and olive pit have tempted him
out here amid the waste, the once lovely city
toiling from the tusk-turned earth
where children stumbled in their ecstasy.
Bitter sat our city in its riches.
Each day passed and we shook our heads
asking had it been a dream as we ached
toward sleep, lean with industry.
The palm trees trembled in the night,
wreathed in reticent music.
The irises have slept the evening dry.
They've shut themselves against our homing steps
and dry still as the world rushes into the chill.

TACKLE

Along the brackish wall
rot crab nets,
cuts of braided line.
A cork squats in the brown water.
Someone's left a trap intact. The clean cord
comes up taut, hauls sixteen fizzing shells
into the unfiltered sun, lets them
swim again so beautifully.
You wander off imagining the crisis
that could leave such fruits unplucked:
a heart attack, dog's death, divorce,
imagining the morning in the birth of June
your father taught you how to crab,
to knot the turkey necks in nylon,
let the nets down through the dark
and give it fifteen minutes,
a good fifteen minutes,
and pull up tenderly, hand over hand,
and shake the shining claws into the bushel.
How they'd menace you, then, raising
pincers to a sky that paled against
the azure of their shells.
That summer saw the record mako caught,
the one that hit a hundred pound tuna
at the midnight lump and bowed the bright rod
not to be unbent till the spool shone
and the knot popped,

feckless as a dandelion root.
And the ragged jaws ranged off
dragging a hundred fathoms' monofilament.
A charter trolled the loose end from the dark,
felt the flickering life, spliced it
to the heavy reel and saw,
hours later in the wasting sun,
the cold blue back, the black eyes
staring as they lashed the body to port
and labored up the heaving green of the Gulf.
The record books won't show its thousand pounds.
But then again it's often that the best
of what we do begins in accident,
in plucking up an unimagined thread
and taking its terrible revelation to the grave
like the hearse you saw later at the sea wall,
its silver snub nose staring over the waves
at a band of sky come round again
like dawn beneath the April storms.

THE BRIDGE

Alone once in the stream of clay,
gasping tender breaths above the lapping.
And the dragon, dripping, wound about the tree,
attributing its fall to wanton locks
until it dried and took its desert way
to dusk among the cedars' fragrance.

Then there swelled a sacrificial fragrance
as flood returned the flesh to clay.
Hardly had the bark got underway
when all the word of water was the lapping
fraught with cancer's drift amid the locks
that billowed with the cubic tree.

The far-off spar took up the bundled tree
and mounted to the fire's fragrance
licking at the lank, long-promised locks.
The screaming cheek was raised from altar clay
while other blood beat thunder out to lapping
to let the cuckold take his hallowed way.

Now the traitor lost his wilder way
and caught his skull upon the sweeping tree.
Iron stalked the oak's grey grasp, iron lapping,
smiling the savor of the desperate fragrance.
No weeping half-relieved could turn the clay
or comb the wrath away from severed locks.

But drunk with love of little as a lock
the potter held the wheel's eternal way
and spread his indiffusion through the clay.
The hammer beat the roses from the tree
which dripped a holocaust of fragrance
to seven soldiers' circlet lapping.

And when the dead descended to the lapping,
teasing out the thorns from dripping locks,
there rose the sweet sub-Templar fragrance,
steeping blood to oversee the way
that struck a dread undoing from the tree
and set a stair for souls of clay.

And we are lapping toward the tendered way,
straining sips from locks along the tree,
surrendering our fragrance to the clay.

KANDINSKY AT THE CLOSING OF AN EYE

You do not have to stay awake
to make a habit of amazement.
Close your eyes.
Sometimes what you tell yourself
can only come by fasts and vigils
in the cold of three o'clock
is waiting at the doorway of a dream.
After all you are the center of a universe.
Once the first unquiet darkness
flickers into eyeless night,
the bodies eclipsed in the course of your orbit
will begin to give you back their shining halos.
Be afraid of the abyss that is yourself.
Whether you are still and silent
or scream the utter dregs of your unease,
it will dismast you with its stare.
This is the upshot of your artlessness,
the ecstasy that says so be it
and begins its steep descent
against the blackness that it trusts.
There hangs the shadowed planet it imagined,
an emptiness too great to be conceived.

NOSTALGIA

The way of the afternoon with the grass
undoes me, deeds my blood to dust
until I feel the flow of night fall
as a stone, as a corpse fresh locusted.
Up comes choral fury in the dusk.
Invisibly the oak trees scream
our breed to dissolution,
and the faces I have known, have touched,
have drifted with to sleep slip by
like bodies marbled in the long
unstinting kisses of a river.
This is not the last of us,
my child with the day's death
like holiness in your hair.
This ache is no false promise.

THE MAN WITH THE BROWN GUITAR

Like a lone banana leaf
aloft to cool a king,
lonely in its wholeness,
in the wind-fondling fullness
of its untorn faces,
he strums the shadowless dusk
above the city.
His is the blinding of the river,
the bitter gusts of coffee and cigars,
the rust tang at his fingertips.
Theirs is the day that is
for us forever, the sun's now
we are made mad to contact,
to come one with.
Let the little world
beyond our rooftop
rattle in the blown away rain.
Let him turn away,
his green hat like a tombstone
melting in the dog day breeze.

PROMISE

Night whispers cool again. Life's set to start
all over. It's just possible, breathing
the sweet moonlight beneath the magnolias,
to think this time we might do nothing wrong.
The sun lies late in space these autumn dawns,
and fish in the dim cold hum of their brains
feel the first faint urge for deep water. Dark
soothes nature like a suffocating breast.
The wear like lean years leaves the birds' voices,
and the sky takes up its shallow, brassy
look like seawater in the gloaming, unraveled
over dead men's shields. Summer's blood is still
in the flowing of the world into time.

THE PAINTER TO HIS MUSE

Was the you that you turned
as I sat as you sat as
you turned and my brush
like a horn stripped the shape
of you from the light
the you that you said could not
no not then not now or yet
say the word that I asked
or were you you who faced
these ways at once there
where we tore that word
from time like me not now
what one could start to say?

ST. FRANCIS AT THE TURNING OF THE YEAR

The maples have begun to ache.
The blood has flowered in their palms
like St. Francis on his rock,
enfolded in the feathers of the seraphs,
like the willowed mystic our El Greco
eyes in skulls of white flame
whispering to lean, lean in
as the fevered world turns
in its sleep toward the cold.

THE ALTAR BOYS' SMOKE BREAK IN PHOTOGRAPHS

Those wings carve terror from the gates
of our painted paradise, screaming unmoved
down the endless air of our empyrean,
Who—Who—Who—Is As He.
Ululeia, ululeia, chant the fallen
in the frigid perfection of their will,
their coral lips creaking
on the vapor of their voices
like crows on their cries in the morning cold.
And his newborn eyes are coals,
and he kisses his cigarette,
swallowing his flaming sword
to thicken incense in the darkness of the temple,
to pause and sigh again what's gone unsaid
since there was what once was not.
And the burning tip flickers
like a bull in the cool of a cave
as they gather countless on the Godhead,
stepping from their cyclone to smoke,
to stare dead into the open eye, unseen.

THE ARTISTS' LAMENT

If only we could start from nothing,
no canvas and no page, no ineluctable
thisness of our art. If only time would strip
space bare and give us back the unsung
of eternity. Splay the white tree.
Shock its pollen into flight against the dark
that pumps our sun like heart's blood
pooled in wonder. Jewel this firmament
in fishhooks, spin it into fruits of
abscess steadying this star's bloom
in their sickness. This is you is you
is nothing but the burning you conceive
when earth upholds your throbbing head.

THE TABLE

This is where we work where we eat
where our coats are hung and our hands
are threaded to the grain of our tools
where our faces ache with labor
in the cold that comes between the boards
where our elbows press the blue incisive
desert where the hunger curls all fetal
in the plates where the fork and the knife
know nothing but the terror in our hands
our wrists our shoulders set askew
our hands curled into claws
to say how long how long how long
until the bough breaks and we build
that sleepless night again from scratch.

STILL LIFE WITH CANDLE

Can a candle keep wide awake
amid the tattered shadows of the dead?
And in its brilliance will this wasteland
wash up any merit, disgorge a gnaw of meat
that still says mine or is there only
I, I, I alone in endless emptiness?

Is it only its own brilliance that the candle
cuts from the gloom like a canvas
crusted in a masquerade of nature?
The sibilance of absence, soft as wings,
wells from the somber city and sustains
our aching sweet suspicion: all is well.

This liquid flame tricks fingers
down my cheek, though, as I turn,
licks at the back of my neck as I
vanish into the still life of my mind.

In, in, mad candle. Keep like blood
that echoes in a skull, seeps through agonies
of olives, seals the nightmare in its sleep,
and cries, oh yes, I see, for this, oh yes, I came.

WHAT YOU DO NOT HAVE

Sleep. Summon this meridian dream
equating world and unworld, you and not you,
the way a baby knows itself
as the ripened breast, the woman
it opened to agony. Only on occasion
will the magic that you daydream
rush forests from the meadow
where you've lain to watch the animals
float their friendly way across the sky.
Only when the unseen world grants
its unasked miracle will the infinite faces
of orchids awaken to the fireflies
dazzling the night like incense
flaming in the stained sun.

SUZANNE'S CAREER

Has the last smoke curdled on her lips
like sea foam on the falling tide?
The dusk is gusting from a thousand years
of unexpected corners where the spark of it
this yes, yes this is it unspoken but splintering
like trumpet blasts in the blood
has leapt like a sun from the cold ground.
Is she waiting for the decent creak
of his step in the pretending house,
where the day will slide pale and smiling
and still a little drunk into the rumple of sheets?
She knew that he would come but still she
waited just for you knowing the groan
of his step in the hall baring her teeth
to the dark he took to be his own.

ELEAZAR AND THE ELEPHANT

When the sun's flood thundered on the shields of bronze
till the mountains shone like fallen moons,
the Indian drivers in battlements
on elephants' backs
cried their untranslatable encouragement.
Drunk with mulberry, ears spread like steadying hands,
the tons of leatherbound blood drummed nightmares
from the city in its sabbath.
And wrath like hope closed over Eleazer
at the kingly armor constellated
on the monster's shoulders.
In their midst he burned like a pagan god,
carving his dark river toward the beast
to pierce its belly. And its death blared
at the brazen sky that seemed to break
upon him, crushing him to the dust
as evening came and the reflective world fell dark.

THE DEATH OF THE ART TEACHER

You loved to show me how to see the world,
how the endlessly divisible things
we spell by rainbow, insect, shark, all curl
inside the silver curves the graphite sings
against the paper's possibility,
how light elides its own soft vanishing.
You bore my blinding inability
and drew me back toward the sun that rings
the triumph of what splinters, crumbles, fades.
I hear your heart, your heart's ease echoing
along the galleries, among the glades,
through silences that time can never bring.
You are again the light below the door
imaging what is in what is no more.

THE KINDNESS OF MEMORY

But those were not the best of all my days,
that June where Newman walked and Campion prayed,
the graveyards where the grey stones turned to gold
as summer suns assumed the light that rolled
across the blue god's foaming beard to send
the bright divines to newborn worlds, to mend
our myth and making. Those were not the last
of wonders to adorn our local past.
Those, it seems, were overture and prelude,
the little things a novice might conclude
were meant to sate the longing after art
that founders in the maelstrom of the heart
more measured to eternity than time,
more taken by the song than by the lime
that reason lays when left to its device.
Still, drift back along the towpath. That slice
of orange gleaming at the pewter rim
set down before you at the Trout, the trim
figures of the riverboats arriving
at the bank below the inn contriving
Edens of the elms and foxgloves planted
when hours, abbeys, and chants recanted
crept from ivy's shade through the dying sun,
that Norman church where hart and peacock run
from dusk to dusk, pursuing into night
the one whose blood bore witness to the light,
could no more number sweetest of my hours

than Adam's dreams in the garden's bowers.
Around the meadow, along the Isis,
where the blue-black swan stroke stirred the crisis
of my gaze on the willow-black water,
memories of you, your eyes and laughter,
raced on before me and rushed up after,
making what perfection I felt the seed
of time that justifies desire to need
and swells silent monuments of longing.
When memories like lilies come thronging
to the whispering shore of what remains
in rushing to the ocean's trackless plains,
they loose their incense to the mystery
of that which, having been, will ever be.

CONJUGATION

For Pip, Ahab, and Starbuck

I see.
You see.
It sees.
You see me seeing me
inside your seeing,
see not me made me
on sight, on strength
of gazes gone mutual
in supple solitude.
You see not you made you
in glancing her and hers in his.
We see each other seeing
who knows how
they see our shared
amazement managed
by the spun tide
spooling time to time
to timeless splicing
of all wheres in one.
I see me mad,
amended
to the mysticetic
mantling
of the end space.
By what we see unseen

you see solely your unseeing,
imagining a magic in these eyes
that cannot cast you back
upon your only shore.
I see. I sing. I cannot chant you
to your dread content,
cannot upend the bell chime
rippling away those eyes
that milked a tear
from the blood tide
curdled in your brow.

SIGNS

There it goes again,
my right hand
off on a frolic of its own.
Not like that.
I'm talking to myself again.
But anyway I'm driving
through City Park, you know
that spot where the road curves
down between the bayou
and the art museum
going thump thump thump
between the pale grey slabs
to pucker up your butt
when this crazy right hand
starts coming up to touch
my forehead like I was
an old lady on the streetcar
going past St. Antony's
except I caught it
before it could go anywhere,
stuck it down hard on the armrest
so it couldn't even if it did want to
like I was a Roman soldier
my beautiful naked body against
a beautiful tree to say
how beautiful you are
stuck full of arrows,

Cupid's pincushion,
and the whole insane world
falling in love with you again.
Do you remember that scene
in Robin Hood Men in Tights
when Mel Brooks rides in
with his load of sacramental wine
and says wait a minute
there's things here.
Well, I don't know when
my right hand saw that movie but
you oughtta see that crazy bastard now.
And now it's not just art museums.
Now it's granite graveyard sculptures.
Now it's crape myrtle clusters
like raspberry sherbet.
Now it's strangers' faces
and garden gnomes
and curious cracks in the sidewalk.
Now it's roach wings
on the kitchen floor
and sweat behind an ear
and the veins that snake
around alabaster knuckles.
I tell him take it down a notch.
I'm tired of the roadkill
and the shining galaxies of flies
and the smiles at the red lights
and the signs that say
anything at all is a blessing.
God, I'm tired.
The poor left hand
hasn't got a clue
what the other's doing.
He's had to learn
to button and zip and wipe

and eat his meals in silence.
And I can't help thinking
this has got to end.
We've got to draw the line somewhere.
I'm starting to feel
like Moira Shearer,
dancing toward
the shrill unstoppable tracks,
till Sunday evening I collapse
on the living room couch
where the tv blazes
nightmares set beyond the sea
smoke to mock all incense
and the blood and the blood
and the blood that never slakes
the war god's tramping boots
and I want to scream
for God's sake,
but he's still at it
as I drift off
thinking
how different it is
from the paintings,
where the artist
won't allow the arrows
their lust, won't let
the lovely body be ripped
from its own amazing nakedness
thinking
yes but
even the murderer
that gnaws away the fingers
and the face cannot make us
quit our love
thinking
even the worst

is still a thing,
here,
a thing
like the trees
and the rocks
and the wind
that cries don't
you look away.

www.ingramcontent.com/pod-product-compliance
Lightning Source LLC
Chambersburg PA
CBHW071730040426
42446CB00011B/2294